To S.
I am so glad you
love to read. I'm
so glad that you were
in my first grade
room at Seiberling School.
Miss Hagstrom

PETER

POLLY

JACK   THOMAS

For Amelia   B.F.

For the Morgans of Talog   D.L.

Text copyright © 1984 by David Lloyd.
Illustrations copyright © 1984 by Barbara Firth.
All rights reserved. Produced for the
publishers by Walker Books Ltd, London. First published in the
United States by Scholastic Inc.

12 11 10 9 8 7 6 5 4 3 2 1   10   5 6 7 8 9 / 8

Printed and bound by
L.E.G.O., Vicenza, Italy

JACK

THE DOG

Written by DAVID LLOYD
Illustrated by BARBARA FIRTH

SCHOLASTIC INC.
New York Toronto London Auckland Sydney

"Today we go west, Jack," Angel said. "There's someone I want you to meet."

They were the best of friends, the old man and his dog.

Angel had always been old, ever since Jack could remember.

He had taught Jack everything.

"Off we go, Jack," Angel said. "Down the bumpetty road again."

"It's not far," Angel said, "just a day and a night away."

In the day Jack sometimes rode in the cart, and sometimes he ran beside Angel.

In the night they slept in the open.

"There's nowhere more grand than the Star Hotel," Angel said, as they lay down.

Life had always been a journey like this, ever since Jack could remember.

When they stopped the next day,
everything was the same as usual at first.
    They got ready for the show.
    "Bow, wow, wow! Whose dog art thou?"
Angel began, when the children arrived.

Jack barked and shook hands with Angel.
This was just the beginning.

With a huge jump, right over Angel's
back, he began the real tricks.

Jack was the cleverest dog in the world.

But after the show it was different.

Angel collected the money, like always, and packed up the cart, like always.

But then he started talking to Jack, stroking him all the time.

"I have to go away on my own now, Jack," he said. "I'm old, and my journey's nearly over. Nothing lasts for ever, Jack, good boy, Jack. Be clever, try to understand."

Slowly Jack understood that Angel was saying goodbye.

They went to a house and met a man.
"This is Mr. Bradley, Jack, you'll have
a good home here. He'll look after you."

It was time for Angel to go.

"Stay, Jack," Angel said. "Good boy."

So Jack stayed, because this was one
of his tricks.

And Angel went away.

There are people who are kind, and other people who pretend to be kind when they want something.

Mr. Bradley only gave Jack a home because he wanted a dog who did tricks.

But when Angel went away, Jack stopped doing tricks.

He pined for the bumpetty road and the Star Hotel. He pined for Angel.

"Bow, wow, wow, Jack!" Mr. Bradley said. "Here, Jack, shake hands!"

Jack just hung his head.

"Stupid dog!" Mr. Bradley said.

He made a rough kennel outside, and tied Jack there.

He brought food for Jack, but not every day.

"Stupidest dog in the world!" Mr. Bradley said, aiming a kick at him.

Now Jack could only lie at the end of his rope, and watch, and wait.

Who was this looking over the wall?
Who was this climbing down?
It was Amy, from next door.
She knew Jack. She had seen Mr. Bradley
kicking Jack. She wanted him to be free.
"Can't you escape, Jack?" she whispered.
"Can't you bite through the rope? Wait,
I'll help you. But don't make a sound,
or Mr. Bradley will come!"

Jack jumped.
He really jumped like
he used to.
He almost jumped into
Amy's arms.
But he didn't make a sound.

Amy couldn't untie Jack's rope and she
didn't have a knife.

So she rubbed the rope on a brick until
it frayed, and then she and Jack pulled
together and the rope broke.

Amy tumbled over backwards.
CRASH! BANG!
She knocked over a bucket and spade.
"Quick, Jack, run!"
Amy sprang up and vanished in an
instant back over the wall.

Mr. Bradley came running.

"Come here, you stupid dog!" he shouted, but of course Jack didn't come. "I'll get you then, and heaven help you when I do!"

Now there was a chase, and Jack used all the tricks he knew. He ran rings round Mr. Bradley, until Mr. Bradley could run no more, and just stood in the yard in a giddy muddle.

Jack jumped in the air again, just for fun.

Then he ran round the shed, through the gap in the fence, and off and away down the bumpetty road.

Amy waved goodbye.

Jack ran and ran.

He ran for many days and many nights.

He slept in the Star Hotel again, and he was happy.

He often thought about Angel.

He felt that Angel was still there, in a way.

Then one day Jack stopped running, not knowing where he was running to.

It was evening.

The stars were coming out.

A mouse and a rabbit were sitting side by side at the edge of the road.

They just looked at Jack.
"Where are you going?"
the rabbit asked.
"Can we come with
you?" the mouse asked.
"Please," the rabbit said.
"We're frightened of the
night," said the mouse.
It was Thomas and Tim.

Jack found out where he was going.
He was going on, that's where, with Tim
and Thomas.
"Don't worry about the night," he said.
"I know the grandest hotel on earth."

There are seven animals in the gang today.
They have all had great escapes.
They live together and travel together.
They are friends.

This evening they are standing on a high
hilltop. It is Jack's turn to tell the story.

"Once upon a time," he begins, "there was
a very wrinkled old man called Angel."

And the story which he tells is the story
in this book.

WALDO   MRS. NOISY   TIM